My Secret Blueprint

Live your life,
Fill this out,
Pass it on as your Legacy Story

Kristine Desrosiers

Hello,

I have filled out this book for you to read and pass down from generation to generation.

I do hope you enjoy reading about me and my life.

Maybe my words will inspire you!

I hope we are similar in the subjects that are important to YOU.

With Love,

____
My Printed Name

____
Date

____
My Signature

Your Legacy Roots Publishing

California

www.mysecretblueprintbook.com

ISBN (ebook) 978-0-9673213-7-0
ISBN (hardback) 978-0-9673213-5-6
ISBN (paperback) 978-0-9673213-4-9

Cover designer: Ridwan Adesina, Polyarts36@gmail.com

Interior designer, illustrator:

Deborah Perdue, https://illuminationgraphics.com

Editor: Margaret A. Harrell, https://margaretharrell.com

Artwork courtesy of Shutterstock.com and Depositphotos.com

DEDICATION

This book is dedicated with all my love to my daughter Shannon

*I want her to know all about me since my mother passed away
before I could find out all about her.*

To my grandchildren and great grandchildren and their children.

May many generations read about the life we lead with hopes

of inspiring you.

In Loving Memory of

*My grandmother Eiri Benson.
By sharing one tidbit of information with me, it inspired me
to create this book.*

My mother, father, grandparents on both sides

CONTENTS

ATTENTION!

*This book is meant to be
filled out in your leisure time.*

When will you have time to fill this out, you ask?

* Morning coffee or tea or after a workout or meditation

* Train, taxi, or bus ride before or after work

* Lunch break or doctor's appointment (while waiting)

* When family members are out of the house, kids napping or asleep
  for the night

* Don't want to watch TV? Wind down and enjoy memories from the past

* Vacation, staycation, business travel or "Me Time"

* Birthdays, anniversaries, family reunions or holiday gatherings or any
  excuse families can get together. Have an older family member share
  with younger family members. They will get a kick out of how much
  alike or not alike they are!

This book is meant to be fun and bring families closer together.

Start the Legacy and pass your story to future generations.

*Maybe your story will become a
Book or Movie someday?*

This is about YOU

Customize it to fit your needs. Add stickers or
draw your own pictures throughout the book. There are blank pages
provided as well.

Savor each chapter and fill in as much as you can remember.
Ask family members for the rest!

Q & A

What if you are single? This book is about <u>YOU</u>. Your family will love it if you share it with them.

What if you are married with no children? You and your spouse/partner can learn more about each other as you fill it out and share.

There is a pregnancy section, and I am a guy! Tear out the pages or skip what doesn't pertain to you. You can also paste another page on top of those pages that you want to share.

I have loved ones that have passed on. Should I still fill out the book for them? What a wonderful tribute to your family! Fill in everything you know and ask other family members for their input. Once you have all the information, you will have fond memories that future generations will cherish.

Bad memories or too many bad memories? That is okay! We all have events from our past that hurt. Talk about those things. You never know . . . it might be good for your soul to get it out and on paper!

New Mom or Dad? If you purchased this book for your child, you might discover how many things you remember about yourself growing up. Maybe buy one for yourself to share with your child/children as they grow up. This book is meant to be fun and bring families closer together.

I do not have pictures of places where I used to live or visit. Do an internet search. Copy and paste them onto the blank pages provided after each chapter.

After I've filled out this book, what do I do? This book provides a fun, creative way for families to learn more about each other. It makes a great communication tool and conversation starter. Are you a parent having a hard time connecting with your child this year? Share something from your book and see if the same or similar experience happened to them. Maybe your child will begin to have a deeper understanding of who you are.

Why are family members either so much alike or so different? Families share similar traits from one generation to the other. Sometimes family members never even know it. Maybe your great grandchild, niece or cousin will be just like you, but no one will ever know unless you write it down! Here is your chance to tell all! Remember, this book is to pass down from generation to generation.

Do you have a family gathering or family reunion coming up? Tell everyone to bring their books and spend time getting to REALLY know each other.

Good or bad, this is your story.

No one had the perfect childhood.

The hard times and rough times make us stronger

and ready for the other challenges life has to offer.

You were born an original don't die a copy

Don't get overwhelmed by the questions.

Look through the chapters, and when you see an easy

question . . . fill it out, then put the book down for a while.

Pick it back up when you are ready to move on.

Customize the pages to fit your needs. Savor each chapter

and fill in as much as you can remember.

When you are done,
you will have your own masterpiece.

Now turn the page, take a deep breath and step back into

your yesteryears and smile.

Let's

begin

your

journey . . .

MY FAMILY TREE

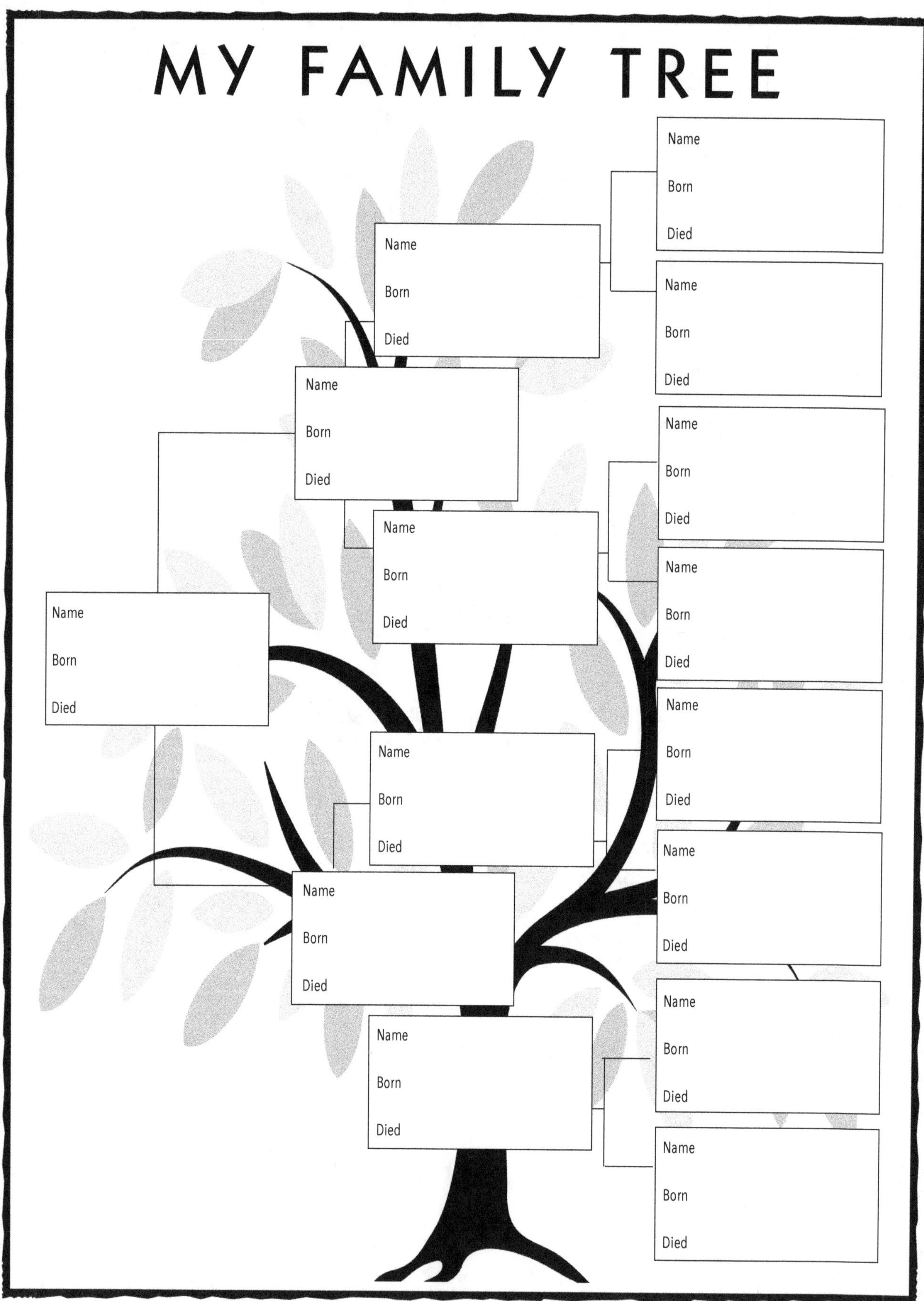

ANCESTRY DNA RESULTS

*There are so many different DNA tests on the market.
Being able to spit in a tube and find out where your relatives
originated from is fascinating! Tell us all about YOU!*

ANCESTRY DNA RESULTS

More about what I find out, information that surprised me the most.

____

____

____

____

____

____

____

____

____

____

____

____

____

____

Babies
are so
precious!

MY FIRST YEAR

You probably don't remember your first year.
This is when you pull out your baby book and start to copy from that.
If your book doesn't have the answers, ask your family if you can.

My name at birth ____

My mom's due date ____

My date of birth _______________________

City _______________________ State _____ County _______________

Country____________ Hospital Name_______________________________

Address____

My mom's labor lasted______ hours

Problems my mom had in labor from what I'm told

____

I have a birthmark(s) ____

My mom's full name ____

My mom's nationality____

My dad's full name____

My dad's nationality___________________________________

My eye color is ___________ in color. My hair is [ ] straight [ ] curly [ ] wavy

My hair color is ______________________

This is what I was told about me when I was born

____

My first baby picture looks more like [   ] Mom [   ] Dad or [   ] someone else

When I first came home, I slept _______ hours at a time

My sleep pattern

____

____

My favorite thing to look at ____

My first tooth came in at _______ months old

I held my own bottle at _______ months old

I rolled from my back to my stomach at _______ months old

I sat up when I was _______ months old

I crawled when I was _______ months old

I started walking when I was _______ months old

My first word was _______________________________

I was _______ months old

Other words I could say____

Soft foods I liked ____

Soft food I didn't like at all! ____

I first drank from a cup when I was _______ months old

I started feeding myself at _______ months old

I ate solid foods when I was _______ months old

First real food I ate ____

I have allergies to ____

Here's a funny story to share about me

____

____

____

____

Games I loved to play ___________________

Songs I loved to hear ___________________

I would laugh so hard when ______________

I would get so upset when _______________

My favorite toy/object/animal was _______

First time I slept through the night I was ___ months old. My family was *So Happy!*

____

My first trip/vacation was to

____

When I was born our address was

____

Guests invited to my first birthday party

____

____

____

MORE TO ADD ABOUT MY FIRST YEAR:
I WAS TOLD . . .

Children are so innocent, they say the funniest things!

A LITTLE ONE GROWING UP . . .

How good is your memory? How far back do your <u>really</u> remember?
Here is your chance to recall your first memory! Enjoy the rest of this
section as you dig back DEEP into your memories.
Get that baby book out again if it was just too early to remember.

My name came from ____

My name means____

My nickname was ____

My earliest memory. I was_______ years old

____

____

____

I was told my personality was (happy, talkative etc.) ________________________

My favorite place to go as a small child

____

My favorite game

____

My favorite toy/object/animal

____

I named my favorite animal/toy/other _______________________________

My favorite outfit ____

My favorite shoes ____

My favorite fruit ____

My favorite foods

____

My favorite candy

____

My favorite drinks

____

I think my "trademark" that made me "me" was

____

The silliest/stupidest thing I ever did when I was young was

____

____

I liked helping my mother with

____

I liked helping my father with

____

When I helped inside the house, I would

____

When I helped outside the house, I would

____

My most serious illness was

____

I was _______ years old

The different kinds of animals I had growing up

Type of animal_________________________   Name ___________________________

Type of animal_________________________   Name ___________________________

Type of animal_________________________   Name ___________________________

Type of animal_________________________   Name ___________________________

My favorite pet was ____

Other important facts you should know

____

____

My favorite sports/activities (listed below)

Sport/Age ____

Sport/Age ____

Sport/Age ____

Sport/Age ____

Notes

____

____

I played these sports/activities too

Sport/Age ____

Sport/Age ____

family is forever
make every
interaction count!

THIS IS MY FAMILY
(WHETHER I LIKE IT OR NOT!)

*Why are family members either so much alike or so different?
Well, here's your chance to tell all! Remember, this book is to pass down from
generation to generation. Maybe one or two generations down from you will be
just like you, but they will never know unless you write it down!*

The language that was spoken in our house was _______________________

Now that I am older, I look more like [   ] Mom [   ] Dad

What famous person do people tell you, you look like?

____

I am an only child (Yes) or (No)

(If you are the only child, did you have a friend who was like your sibling?)
There is also a separate friend's section further down.

I have______ brothers and _______ sisters

Their names are

____

____

I am the oldest/middle/youngest_________________________________

I used to get along best with _______________________________

I used to get along least with _______________________________

The things we liked to do together as kids was

____

____

____

The hardest I ever laughed was when _______________________________

The silliest/stupidest thing we ever got away with was

____

____

The best secret (I/we) hid from our family was

____

____

I [   ] (did [   ] did not ever tell my family

The best dish my mom cooked was _______________________________

The best dish my dad cooked was _______________________________

When we went out to eat as a family, we usually went to

____

My favorite meal to order was_______________________________

My favorite thing that we did as a family was

____

____

Our favorite vacations were

____

____

The best vacation story was

____

____

____

The worst vacation story was

____

____

____

____

We didn't really go on vacation yearly. What we did was

____

____

____

TRADITIONS

Our family likes to celebrate this event each year_______________________

____

This event was important to my family because

____

____

____

An annual tradition we did as a family was

____

____

____

Our family's favorite holiday was _______________________________

This is what we did for that holiday

____

____

____

My favorite relative was ______________________________

What I love the best about this relative was

____

____

____

Let me tell you about my other family members I truly care about

____

____

____

Holidays we liked to celebrate

____

____

____

We [   ] do [   ] do not have Family Reunions

MORE TO ADD ABOUT MY FAMILY

No one can replace an
Aunt, Uncle, Cousin or
Grandparent

They are Priceless

GRANDPARENTS

*Being a grandparent is the best feeling in the world,
but being a grandchild has its benefits too!
Tell us about yours!*

Mom's Parents

Grandmother (my name for her) ___________________________________

Let me tell you about her

____

____

____

____

Grandfather (my name for him) ___________________________________

Let me tell you about him

____

____

____

____

This is our oldest relative on my mom's side. They are _______ years old

The fondest memory I have

____

____

____

____

Dad's Parents

Grandmother (my name for her) _______________________________

Let me tell you about her

____

____

____

____

Grandfather (my name for him) _______________________________

Let me tell you about him

____

____

____

____

This is our oldest relative on my dad's side. They are _______ years old

The fondest memory I have

____

____

____

____

AUNTS, UNCLES AND COUSINS

*Being around these relatives, you will really see your parents
through them, or will you?*

My aunts' names

____

I called my aunts

____

My fondest memory of them

____

____

____

My uncles' names

____

I called my uncles

____

My fondest memory of them

____

____

____

My favorite cousin's name _______________________

A couple of the fondest memories I have of her/him/them

____

____

MORE TO ADD ABOUT MY GRANDPARENTS, AUNTS, UNCLES AND COUSINS

Your life
can be
inspiring
to others

WOW! YA MEAN I WAS ADOPTED!

When you were born, your mom and dad wanted to do the right thing. Even if that meant being selfless and entrusting you to another family so you could have a better life.

Remember . . . being adopted means, "A family wanted YOU so much."

I blessed my new family with ME when I was _______ days/months/years old

My adopted mother and father's names are

____

____

I have ____ brothers and ____ sisters

Their names are

____

____

This is how I feel being adopted

____

____

____

____

____

I found out I was adopted when I was ____ years old

The reason I was put up for adoption was

____

____

ABOUT MY BIRTH FAMILY
(SINCE BEING ADOPTED)

My birth mothers' name _______________________________________

My birth mom lives in ____

I [   ] have [   ] have not been in contact with my birth mom

My birth fathers' name ____

My birth dad lives in ____

I [   ] have [   ] have not been in contact with my birth dad

I was able to find them through

____

____

I was _____ years old when I first found them

I was _____ years old when I first met them

I [   ] do [   ] do not get along with my birth parents

I look more like my [   ] birth mom [   ] birth dad______ [   ] nothing like either

Here are my traits from my biological mom

____

____

Here are my traits from my biological dad

____

____

I found out that I have brothers and sisters, whose names are

____

____

____

____

The names of my grandparents, aunts, uncles, cousins in my biological family are

____

____

____

I [was] [was not] able to find out my genetic/medical history related to my birth parents

Here is some medical information that I found out about my birth family

____

____

____

____

____

[ ]   I am excited about meeting my birth parents
[ ]   I am nervous about meeting my birth parents
[ ]   I don't care
[ ]   I don't want to meet my birth parents
[ ]   I don't want to get disappointed

When I get married and want to start a family of my own, I [ ] will [ ] will not consider adoption.

MORE TO ADD ABOUT MY BIRTH FAMILY

MORE TO ADD ABOUT BEING ADOPTED
I WOULD LIKE TO SHARE

YES, I AM A FOSTER CHILD

*It is hard enough being a child. It is even harder being a foster child.
<u>You are the Heroes of our time</u>. You have gone through so much
that most people will never go through.*

Remember . . . <u>You are</u> one of the Heroes of all time!

I went into the foster system at age ____

I was in the system for____ years.

I was placed in ____ foster home(s)

I liked being in this temporary foster home very much. Let me tell you about it

____

____

____

I made these new friends while in foster care

____

I [   ] was [   ] was not placed permanently

I went back to my family after being in the foster system _____ weeks/months/
years

When I get married and want to start a family of my own, I [   ] will [   ] will not
consider taking in a foster child

This was my experience being a foster child that I want to share

____

____

____

MORE TO ADD ABOUT BEING A FOSTER CHILD

HOME IS A PLACE TO FEEL SAFE AND WARM

HOME SWEET HOME

What kind of place did you grow up in? Was it a house or an apartment?
A high-rise in the city? In the suburbs or on a farm?
Whatever and wherever it was, it was home.
Let's go back there in your mind and relive some of those days.

These are the cities/states I lived in, growing up

____

____

The first address I remember was

City _______________________________ State ________ Zip ___________

It was [   ] an apartment [   ] Townhouse [   ] Condo [   ] House ____________

My home I remember had an [   ] attic [   ] basement [} neither

My home I remember was _________________________________ in color

It was built of [   ] wood [   ] brick [   ] concrete [   ] stucco siding

My favorite secret hiding place was

____

The scariest room in the house was

____

My favorite room was

____

I [   ] had my own room [   ] did not have my own room

I had to share it with _________________________________

Let me tell you a story about sharing my room!

____

This is how I decorated my room

____

I had this one favorite thing in my room, and it was

____

The chores I was responsible doing were

____

The way I tried to get out of doing these chores was

____

____

We [   ] had [   ] did not have many of my friends over to my home

Let me tell you how many kids were at our house and what we would do

____

____

We had these events on our streets, growing up

____

____

What I remember most about my favorite neighborhood I grew up in was

____

This is what I think about today's neighborhoods that are different from when I was growing up

____

=

MORE TO ADD ABOUT HOME SWEET HOME

*All people's God
is special to them*

RELIGION

Religion can be a very private and personal issue. If you like, share with your future family members how you feel. If this is not a section that feels comfortable for you to describe on paper, by all means pass on it.

To me, "religion" means

____

____

____

I was raised in this religion (faith) _____________________________________

Today, my religion (failth) is ____

I would consider myself [   ] very religious,   [   ] somewhat religious,   [   ] not very religious,   [   ] agnostic,   [   ] atheist

My religion [   ] was [   ] was not separate from my parents' religion

My parents' religion: Mom: _________________ Dad: _________________

I went to church   [   ] Often   [   ] Not Often Enough!

I went to church on these days ____

[   ] I taught Sunday School [   ] I studied to become a priest/pastor/bishop/teacher

I participated in different community-service projects to help other people

Those projects were

____

____

____

I donated my time

____

____

The church mission trips I went on were to

____

____

I enjoyed this mission trip the most!

____

____

____

Date (s) of my mission trips

____

The part of religion I enjoyed the most, growing up, was

____

____

The part of religion I least enjoyed, growing up, was

____

____

The most valuable thing I learned from religion was

____

____

Religion has taught me

____

____

MORE TO ADD ABOUT RELIGION

friends forever

Friends are
like family,
they are
priceless

MY FRIENDS . . . MY YOUNGER YEARS

Having friends is truly a blessing.
Where would we be on those days or nights when we need someone
to talk to and our family just wouldn't understand?
Here's your chance to share and vent!

As I was growing up, my best friend was ________________________________

I met my best friend when I was _______ years old

My childhood friends' names were

____

____

As I got a little older, I hung out with

____

____

I met her/him/them around age _______

Our favorite thing to do together was

____

____

With my childhood friends, the places I used to play the most was

____

____

We enjoyed talking about

____

____

Our best-kept secret was

____

____

The biggest fib/lie we ever got away with was

____

____

We used to pretend we

____

____

When we saw each other, this is what we would do

____

____

When we talked about the future, we said

____

____

What I liked most about these friends was

____

____

The best thing we ever did together was

____

____

Traditions we had each year

____

____

[ ] We still keep in touch   [ ] We haven't seen each other in years!

[ ] We correspond through   [ ] We correspond every holiday

MORE TO ADD ABOUT MY FRIENDS

My Hobbies
and Interests
Keep me
SANE!

BOY, I'M TALENTED!

*Everyone loves to create. It is a great feeling of accomplishment
knowing that you made something for yourself or for someone else
with your own hands, mind, spirit and soul.
Did you participate in sports, music or crafts?
Well, here is your chance to show off your personal talents!*

Hobbies

My favorite hobby is

____

____

I found out my least-favorite hobby is

____

____

Other hobbies I have tried are

____

____

____

The best thing I ever did with my hobby was

____

____

____

Because of my hobby

____

____

____

Music and Instruments

The musical instrument(s) I learned is/are

____

____

I learned this instrument because [   ] I really wanted to [   ] My parents made me

This is where I played my instruments

____

____

____

Because of my love for music

____

____

____

My favorite type of music

____

____

____

The music I listened to growing up

____

____

____

My favorite musical group(s)

____

____

My favorite song(s)

____

____

____

My favorite singer(s)

____

____

____

When I hear this or these songs, it takes me back to

____

____

____

Sports/Activities

The sports activity/activities I was most involved in was/were

____

____

My team(s) names

____

____

____

Our best win was

____

____

____

Here is a great story that I have to tell you!

____

____

____

This is who inspired me to get into this sport/activity

____

____

____

Other things you might not know about me with my sports that I want to tell you!

____

____

____

____

____

____

____

____

____

____

Hunting

*Hunting was an integral part of daily life a long time ago.
The reason we hunt is for food, protection, sport or to remove
an animal that is a threat to livestock or farms.*

I (liked) (loved) (did not like) hunting for (type of animal)

____

This is who taught me to hunt

____

The kind of animals I would hunt

____

____

I have gone hunting with

____

____

This is where I would normally hunt

____

____

I also hunted in these different locations

____

____

My favorite hunting story is

____

____

____

Fishing

Fishing was also was an integral part of daily life a long time ago.
Fishing is a great food source and even a competitive sport!

I (liked) (loved) (did not like) fishing

This is who taught me to fish

____

The kind of fish I would catch

____

____

I have gone fishing with

____

____

This is where I would normally fish

____

____

____

I also fished in these different locations

____

____

MY FAVORITE FISHING STORY WAS . . .
AND IT'S A BIG ONE!

I am a Collector

I am a collector of ____

I started collecting when I was _______________________________________

My most prized collection is

____

____

____

____

Cars / Trucks

My very first vehicle____

This vehicle, I have always dreamed of getting

____

I have had these different vehicles

____

____

This was my favorite ____

I also restore cars. Let me tell you about that!

____

____

Let me tell you about my vehicles

____

____

MORE TO ADD ABOUT MY HOBBIES AND INTERESTS

DON'T STOP
IN ANYTHING
YOU DO

Activities I participated in—Mark with a "P"
Activities I liked to watch—Mark with a "W"

Acting
Archery
Badminton
Ballet
Band
Barrel Racing
Baseball
Basketball
Bull Riding
Calf Roping
Cooking
Croquet
CrossFit
Cycling
Dancing
Dart team
Dirt Bike Riding
Disc Jockey
Fencing
Fishing
Football
Gymnastics
Hockey
Horseback Riding
Hunting
Jazz
Jet skiing
Jewelry Making
Juggling
Kayaking
Kick Boxing
Making Movies
Marathon races
Martial Arts
Modeling
Origami Artwork
Paintball
Paragliding
Photography

Ping Pong
Playing an Instrument
Pottery
Puppetry
Racquetball
Robotics
Rock Climbing
Rodeo Riding
Roller Blading
Rowing (on a team)
Running
Sailing
Scuba
Sculpting
Singing (in a choir)
Skating
Skiing
Snorkeling
Snowboarding
Soccer
Softball
Speed Skating
Squash
Steer Wrestling
Surfing
Swimming
Tai Chi
Tap Dancing
Tennis
Track
Trick Roping
Volleyball
Wake Boarding
Water Polo
Wine Making
Woodwork or Wood Carving
Writing
Yoga (instructor)
Zumba (instructor)

MORE TO ADD ABOUT ACTIVITIES
I WANT TO SHARE

EASY, KIND, GOOD, GROOVY, CALM VIBES ONLY . . .

THE BEST WAY TO DESCRIBE ME

Circle all the ones that pertain to you

Ambitious	Idealistic
Analytical	Intuitive
Angry	Inventive
Anxious	Joyful
Anxious	Joyous
Artistic	Lazy
Book-smart	Meticulous
Calm/Collected	Motivated
Certain	Motivating
Charming	Neat
Comical	Optimistic
Compassionate	Perceptive
Confident	Pessimistic
Content	Realistic
Controlling	Sarcastic
Crafty	Secure
Creative	Sensible
Cunning	Serious
Curious	Sloppy
Determined	Stable
Dynamic	Stressed
Empowered	Stubborn
Enthusiastic	Studious
Excited	Tenacious
Fearful	Trusting
Focused	Vibrant
Goofy	Wise
Grateful	Witty
Happy	Worrywart
Headstrong	

MORE TO ADD ABOUT THE BEST WAY TO DESCRIBE ME

ONCE <u>YOU</u>

BELIEVE

YOU CAN DO ANYTHING—

<u>YOU CAN!</u>

MY DESIRES

What have you always longed for to do in life? What would you dream about that would bring so much enjoyment and satisfaction to you? Have you started on your desires yet?

When I was very young, my fervent desire was

____

____

When I was growing up, my greatest desire was

____

____

I also really wanted to do

____

____

But......I was too afraid to

____

____

I was not afraid at all to

____

____

As I got older, I realized I really wanted to

____

____

MY DREAMS

A dream is what we want to make come true in our everyday lives.
We all have dreams that we want to fulfill one day.
What do you dream about? Have you started fulfilling those dreams yet?

I have always dreamed about

____

____

____

I tried my dream but then stopped because

____

____

____

I picked up my dream again and this is what happened

____

____

____

I [   ] did fulfill [   ] am fulfilling my dream! Let me tell you about it!

____

____

____

CHALLENGES

Aww . . . challenges . . . part of our everyday life . . .
If we did not have challenges, then who would we be?

I have had these challenges so far in my life

____

____

____

These challenges made me

____

____

____

Because of these challenges, I was able to

____

____

____

What I have learned from these challenges so far

____

____

____

____

____

MORE TO ADD ABOUT MY DREAMS, DESIRES AND CHALLENGES

You are a

HERO

to a lot of people
you have never met

MENTORS

Who is yours? Mentors are those people whom you really admire
as a model, a predecessor, a trailblazer
or whom you aspire to be an even better version of . . .
Who was that person for you?

My mentor growing up was

____

____

My mentor now is

____

____

Lessons I have learned so far from the mentors in my life

____

____

____

____

How I want to help people as a mentor

____

____

____

____

AFFIRMATIONS

I [ ] did [ ] did not grow up with positive affirmations

These affirmations, or positive sayings, were taught to me or I taught them
to myself

____

____

____

____

My view on life is that [} Cup is half full [ ] Cup is half empty

I view life [ ] positively [ ] negatively [ ] other

Describe:

____

____

____

____

Now that I am grown up, these affirmations are important to me. This is how I
integrate them into my life

____

____

____

____

GRATITUDE LIST

I [ ] did [   ] did not write in a gratitude journal

This is how I feel about a Gratitude Journal

____

____

____

MY BUCKET LIST

No matter how young or old you are, all of us have something in our life we want to do before we get too old to do it. Tell us what you have in mind.

When I was young, I wanted to

____

____

Then I realized I really wanted to

____

____

This is what I have done on my bucket list, and I am so glad I did!

____

____

My number-one bucket-list item of what I still really want to do is

____

____

MORE TO ADD MENTORS,
AFFIRMATIONS,
GRATITUDE AND MY BUCKET LIST

Summertime . . .
Put all your cares
and worries away
for another day!

THE GOOD OL' SUMMERTIME!

"No more pencils, no more books. No more teachers' dirty looks."
In the old days, kids everywhere would sing this song.
School was out for the summer!
Let's go back and relive the summers you spent growing up.

When I was younger, I normally did this during my summer break

____

____

____

As I got older, I normally did this during my summer break

____

____

____

When I stayed at home, on a typical day, I would

____

____

____

The best summer I can remember was

____

____

____

My favorite things to do with my friends in the summer were

____

____

____

When it was hot, we cooled off by

____

____

____

We thought it would be fun to re-enact [   ] TV shows [   ] TV commercials [   ] movies [   ] actors' roles [   ] plays [   ] musicals [   ] bands [   ] videos [   ] family memories.

This is what we would do

____

____

____

Other fun things we all did were

____

____

As a family, we spent our vacations

____

____

My favorite family trip was

____

____

____

Our funniest family vacation story was

____

____

____

____

____

____

Some different vacation spots I visited during the summer were

____

____

____

____

____

____

MORE TO ADD ABOUT MY SUMMERS

Winter is the
coziest
time of year

WAS YOUR WINTER A WONDERLAND?

*Whether you spent your winters on the sunny beaches in Florida or skiing down the
snow-topped mountains in Colorado, they are our own set of memories.
Which ones are yours?*

I [ ] Liked [ ] Loved [ ] Hated the snow

The most snow I have ever seen was _______ inches/feet high

The coldest weather I have ever been in _________________________ city/state

We used to build ____

____ in the snow

The average temperature during the winter was __________

My favorite thing to do in the snow was

____

____

My favorite place to ski was

____

My favorite place to snowboard was

____

My favorite place to sled was

____

____

We had snowmobiles and we would take them out to

____

Other snow machines that we had

____

My favorite thing to do in the winter was

____

If there was no snow:

This is what I usually did in the winter

____

____

The type of winter activities I would participate in included the following

____

We would travel to locations with snow, and this is where we would go

____

My favorite thing to do in the winter was

____

____

My favorite winter trip was

____

____

These are the different places I got to see during winter

____

____

MORE TO ADD ABOUT MY WINTERS

You can do Anything You are Motivated to do

COOKING & MY FAVORITE RECIPES

This is who taught me to cook ____

I [   ] liked [   ] loved [   ] did not like cooking

My signature dish ____

____

My favorite foods to cook____

____

____

____

I do not cook; I just show up and chew. Let me tell you who cooked in my

household ____

This is who cooks in our house now _______________________________________

GARDENING

I have been gardening for ____

Let me tell you about my garden and my favorites

____

____

____

EXERCISE

I [ ] enjoy [ ] do not enjoy exercise

My favorite exercise is

____

____

I exercise this much per week

____

This is what I do when I exercise

____

____

____

I love exercise so much, I

____

____

Now that I am older, I realized exercise is good for your body and has many health benefits. This is what I do now:

____

____

____

MORE TO ADD ABOUT COOKING, GARDENING & EXERCISE

Movies & TV shows
can be so inspirational.
Life would be so boring
without them.

BINGE-WATCHING TV

Netflix, Hulu, Prime Video, YouTube, YouTube TV,
Disney, Philo, Fubo, Sling, HBO, AT&T TV

Whew!! So many channels, so little time!
Tell us how you spent your time streaming . . .

My (TV/computer) channels of choice

____

____

I am embarrassed to say, I loved binge watching these shows

____

____

____

This was my favorite show _________________________

This turned out to be my least favorite show _________________________

____

The longest time I binged watched a show was _________________________

The food/snacks I like to eat _________________________

The room I was normally in watching was _________________________

These are all of the shows I watched. Can't believe I watched all of those episodes!!!

____

____

____

MOVIES

In 1905, the first nickelodeon theatre opened in Pittsburgh, Pennsylvania—a five-cent-admission movie theater. Now going to the movies is such a luxury. You can go during the day or night, order food and drinks and sometimes even fall asleep! HA!

My favorite movie of all time ______________________________

My top favorite movies

____

____

Movies I grew up on

____

____

Movies I watched with my parents

____

____

Movies I watched with my friends

____

____

____

____

Movies I watched with my kids

____

____

The name of my neighborhood movie theater

____

____

My favorite snack at the movies

____

____

When I was growing up, it cost $ _______ to see a movie

If we didn't go to the movies close by, this is where we would go to

____

____

POLITICAL VIEWS

Left, Right, Moderate, Independent!
Whichever your views are, write them down below.
Your family sure would like to know how you feel about
the world you live in today.

This is the political party I belong to _______________________________

This is the political party I changed to and why

____

____

____

These are the politicians I have voted for in the past: year / candidates name

____

____

____

____

This is what I want to talk about that's going on in the political world today

____

____

____

____

PROTESTING

Protesting is an expression of what we want to change.
What do you want to change in the world?

I [ ] have [ ] have not ever protested with a group in public

These are the different causes I protested about

____

____

____

This is why I protest

____

____

____

Let me tell you about one protest that stood out in my mind

____

____

____

I prefer to express my views on change or the status quo in a different way.
For instance

____

____

____

MORE TO ADD ABOUT POLITICS
AND PROTESTING

You are

only young

once . . .

SCHOOL DAYS, SCHOOL DAYS

Growing up, you spent five days a week in school.
Tell us everything you can remember.
If you were homeschooled, let us know!

KINDERGARTEN:

The name of my school ____

I was homeschooled [ ] Yes [ ] No

Is your school still there? [ ] Yes [ ] No

My teacher's name ____

My best friend(s) name in kindergarten ____

My other friends names ____

____

Field trips we went on

____

____

ELEMENTARY:

The name of my school ____

I was homeschooled [   ] Yes [   ] No

Years I was homeschooled ____

Is your school still there? [   ] Yes [   ] No

My teacher's name

____

Names of my other teachers and the subjects they taught

____

____

____

My favorite books were ____

____

My favorite subjects were ______________________________________

____

The classes and electives I took were

____

____

I finally got a cell phone when I was _______ years old

I finally got an iPad/Android/laptop when I was _______ years old

My best friend was ____

This is how I met my best friend

____

____

____

These are the names of my friends ______________________________

____

I had a crush on ____

This is who had a crush on me __________________________________

These are the different activities /clubs I was in during my elementary school years

____

____

One of the best stories to tell about elementary school was

____

____

____

JUNIOR HIGH:

The name of my school was _______________________________________

I was homeschooled [   ] Yes [   ] No

Years I was homeschooled ______________

Is your school still there? [   ] Yes [   ] No

My favorite teacher's name _______________________________________

Names of my other teachers and the subjects they taught

____

____

My favorite books were

____

____

____

____

____

The classes and electives I took in school were

____

____

I finally got a cell phone when I was ______ years old

I finally got an iPad/Android/laptop when I was ______ years old

My best friend was ____

This is how I met my best friend

____

____

____

These are the names of my friends

____

____

____

I had a crush on ____

This is who had a crush on me __________________________________

The different activities/clubs I was in during my junior high school years were

____

____

One of the best stories to tell while I was in junior high school was

____

____

HIGH SCHOOL:

The name of my school was ____

I was homeschooled [   ] Yes [   ] No

Years I was homeschooled____________

Is your school still there? [   ] Yes [   ] No

My favorite teacher was ____

Names of my other teachers and the subjects they taught

____

____

My favorite books were

____

____

The classes and electives I took in school were

____

____

____

____

I had these cell phones

____

I had these iPad/Android/laptops

____

I broke my phone or cracked my screen. Here are some funny stories to share

____

____

____

____

My best friend was ____

This is how I met my best friend

____

____

____

____

These are the names of my friends _______________________________

____

I had a crush on ____

This is who had a crush on me ___________________________________

____

The different activities/clubs I belonged to during high school were

____

____

In school, _________________________________ was my favorite subject.

In school, _________________________________ was my least-favorite subject

After school I usually would

____

____

____

In high school, I worked at ____

and got ____________ an hour wage

On weekends, I normally

____

____

____

My hangout was

____

____

I went to my junior prom when I was _______ years old

I went with ____

This is where we went and what we did for my junior prom

____

____

____

I went to my senior prom when I was _______ years old

I went with ____

This is where we went and what we did for my senior prom

____

____

One of the best stories to tell while I was in high school was

____

____

I received this (these) as my graduation gift(s)

____

____

Our high-school graduation trip was to _______________________

I [ ] did [ ] did not go on the trip

After high-school graduation, I

____

____

My plans for the rest of my life then were

____

____

I ended up not going to college, and this is why

____

____

MORE TO ADD ABOUT MY SCHOOL DAYS

BECOME THE PERSON THAT EVERYONE YOU MEET WANTS TO BECOME

COLLEGE!

No more Mom and Dad! I can stay up as late as I want. I don't have anyone telling me what to do, and I can eat all of the junk food I want! Hey?! Mom? Dad? Can YOU send me some MONEY?! NOW!!

I started college in ___________________________________

and graduated in ___________________________________

The name(s) of the college(s) I went to was (were)

____

____

The year my college was established was ___________________________________

My college was located in

____

____

____

I took these classes as a freshman

____

____

____

I took these classes as a sophomore

____

____

I took these classes as a junior

____

____

I took these classes as a senior

____

____

My major was _______________________________________

I decided to change majors and go into

____

____

____

I got as far as [ ] Graduate [ ] Undergraduate [ ] Masters [ ] Ph.D.

My final major and degree were in

____

____

____

The cost annually to attend school was $ _______________________

I [ ] did [ ] did not live on campus

I had some really memorable teachers; some of my favorites were

____

____

My favorite teacher in college was ________________________________

The sorority/fraternity I belonged to was

____

My sorority sisters / fraternity brothers I shared a house with

____

I did not belong to a sorority/fraternity, but my roommate's names were

____

My friends and I always hung out at

____

These are the names of my friends I hung out with

____

____

I had many friends, but my very closest was ____________________

The make of my car in college was ____________________________

In college, I worked at____

and got _______ an hour wage

The different places I worked at

____

____

The funniest story I can remember while I was working was

____

____

Is it Friday Yet?
What do you mean I
work the weekends!

I OWE, I OWE, SO OFF TO WORK I GO!

Being an adult is great! What's not so great is that you can't have the finer things in life unless you have a job. Tell us how your career started.

After graduating, my ambition was to _______________________________

____

____

____

____

After graduating, I owed _________________ in college loans

After graduating, I worked at

____

____

____

The first job I had that paid me a full-time salary was

____

____

____

My first car that I bought on my own was

____

____

I bought it [ ] New [ ] Used

When I did buy a new car, my first one was _______________________

and the cost was $ _______________

When I started, my career goal was to

____

____

____

The best place I ever worked was

____

My job there was _______________________________

The worst place I ever worked was (boy, I'm glad I'm not doing that anymore!)

____

____

____

My favorite boss's name was ____________________

My favorite co-worker was ______________________

My biggest triumph ever on the job was

____

____

____

At work, I was good at

____

____

____

On the other hand, I wasn't so good at

____

____

The easiest job I had was

____

____

____

The most difficult job I had was

____

____

____

If I were to have my fantasy job, it would be

____

____

____

I may have missed the boat in my career when

____

____

____

When I retire, I would like to

____

____

____

MORE TO ADD ABOUT WORKING

**Life will
always
be tough,
but you are
<u>tougher</u>
than that!**

FINALLY! OUT ON MY OWN!

Ya mean I get to leave my clothes laying around <u>my house</u> as long as I want?!?!
(Only if you <u>didn't</u> have a roommate!)

I was _______ years old when I left home

When I left home, I moved to

____

____

____

My first rental cost me $ _______ a month

This is how I furnished it

____

____

____

[   ] I loved living by myself   [   ] I prefer living with a roommate

The best experience living by myself was

____

____

____

My roommate was _________________________________

How I met my roommate

____

____

We got along [ ] well [ ] okay [ ] poorly

What I liked about my roommate was

____

____

____

What bugged me about my roommate was

____

____

____

The biggest fight we ever had was

____

____

____

The most fun we had was

____

____

____

MORE TO ADD ABOUT
BEING ON MY OWN

Yeah...I rock.

I am a

HERO

to many.

MILITARY INFORMATION

If you didn't serve, pass on by.
If you did, company halt! Tell us about your time in uniform.

I served in the ____

I was in the military for _______ years

I [ ] Volunteered [ ] Drafted and entered the service on _______________

I received basic training at

____

____

____

I received special training at

____

____

____

I was first stationed at _______________________________

I served in these different cities, states, countries

____

____

____

My serial # and rank were _______________________________

The assignment I liked the most was

____

____

____

The assignment I liked the least was

____

____

____

The most dangerous thing I ever did in the military was

____

____

____

The names of my closest friends I served with

____

____

____

My rank on separation was

____

Overall, I thought my time in the military was

____

____

____

____

____

MORE TO ADD
ABOUT BEING IN THE MILITARY

BE
the reason
someone
Smiles
back at you

MY FRIENDS . . . ALL GROWN UP

Although being a young adult is a lot of responsibility, it is also the greatest time in your life to experience interacting with different types of personalities. There are so many wonderful people from different backgrounds around the world. Here are some of those memories.

My closest friends

____

____

My friends and I would hang out at

____

____

The weirdest one in our group ___________________________

Once, he/she

____

____

The craziest one in our group

____

Once, he/she

____

____

____

The funniest thing we ever did together

____

____

____

We would spend our summers at

____

____

____

We would spend our winters at

____

____

____

Let me tell you another great story about my wonderful friends and me

____

____

____

____

____

____

____

____

MORE TO ADD ABOUT "MY FRIENDS . . . ALL GROWN UP"

Love
is a
beautiful
thing

WEDDING BELLS!

Now here's your chance to tell all—we want to hear it!

How I met the love of my life

____

____

____

What attracted me to him/her

____

____

____

What I liked most about

____

____

____

We dated for _________________ months/years before getting engaged

We had the most fun when we

____

____

____

We were engaged for _______________ months/years

We were married on

____

____

____

Here is who was in our wedding party

____

____

____

Plans for the wedding went (well/poorly—describe)

____

____

____

The biggest problem was

____

____

____

There were _____________ people who attended our wedding

My favorite wedding story is

____

____

____

We spent our honeymoon at

____

____

____

The first place we lived was in

____

____

____

What our first place looked like

____

____

____

We got our first house in ___________ (year)

We paid for our first house with help from

____

____

____

Our first piece of furniture was ________________________________

We were so excited about owning a home, but there were some not-so-exciting times. Let me tell you both

____

____

____

____

____

THIS IS WHAT PARENTING LOOKS LIKE

MY CHILDREN

*Every parent knows that being a parent can be heavenly . . .
take this chance to tell it all.
The wonderful, the woeful and even the wacky.*

We talked about having _______ child(ren)

We were blessed with _______ child(ren)

We [   ] adopted [   ] did not adopt any children

We raised [   ] foster children [   ] did not raise foster children

Our wonderful child(ren's) name(s)

____

____

____

During my pregnancy, I craved

First Child ____

Second Child ____

Third Child ____

Fourth Child ____

I did or did not get sick during my pregnancy

First Child ____

Second Child ____

Third Child _______________________________________

Fourth Child _______________________________________

My moods were overall

____

____

____

I was sick for weeks/months

First Child _______________________________________

Second Child _______________________________________

Third Child _______________________________________

Fourth Child _______________________________________

I gained this much weight during my pregnancy

First Child _______________________________________

Second Child _______________________________________

Third Child _______________________________________

Fourth Child _______________________________________

I had these problems during my pregnancy

First Child ____

Second Child ____

Third Child ____

Fourth Child ____

Names we picked

Boy ____

Girl ____

The funniest part of my pregnancy was when

First Child

____

____

____

Second Child

____

____

____

Third Child

____

____

____

Fourth Child

____

____

____

It was so exciting having a child, but having all these emotions all at once can be overwhelming. Here are some of my thoughts when you were just born.

____

____

____

____

____

____

When I brought you home from the hospital, we had quite a time. Let me tell you!

First Child _______________________________________

____

Second Child _____________________________________

____

Third Child _______________________________________

____

Fourth Child ______________________________________

____

When I was raising my child(ren), times were

____

____

____

The golden rule I taught my child(ren) was

____

____

____

Now my child(ren) live(s)

____

____

____

I get to see them/him/her

____

____

____

Single *Vibes* Only

OKAY, I'M A SINGLE PARENT...NOW WHAT?!

Being a single parent has its struggles but others really enjoy their freedom. During this time is when we figure out a lot about ourselves that we may have forgotten.

We separated in the month/year _______________________

Our divorce was final, month/year _______________________

We [　] did [　] did not have a good relationship after we divorced

I had [　] Full [　] 50/50 [　] Partial custody of my child(ren) and here was our arrangement

____

____

____

____

____

____

While I was a single parent, we did these different activities when we were together

____

____

____

____

____

____

____

____

____

My best memory about being a single parent

____

____

____

____

____

____

____

These were my challenges while being a single parent

____

____

____

____

____

____

____

____

MORE TO ADD ABOUT BEING
A SINGLE PARENT

MY SECOND MARRIAGE

We don't always know if it is going to be "Happily Ever After" the first time.
It's great that people can share their lives with another
Special someone and have more wonderful children.

[ ] I am divorced   [   ] am a widow/widower

My wonderful husband's name is______________________________________

My stepchild(ren's) name(s) is/are

____

____

____

We have been married for _________ years

We have ________ child(ren) together

Our child(ren's) name(s) is/are

____

____

We first talked about having _______ child(ren)

We had _______ child(ren) together

We [ ] adopted [   ] did not adopt any children

We raised [   ] foster children [   ] did not raise foster children

During my pregnancies in this marriage, I craved

First Child

____

____

Second Child

____

____

Third Child

____

____

I did or did not get sick during my pregnancy in this marriage

First Child

____

____

Second Child

____

____

Third Child

____

____

My moods were overall

____

____

____

I was sick for ________ weeks/months

First Child ______________________________________

Second Child ____________________________________

Third Child _____________________________________

I gained this much weight during my pregnancy

First Child ______________________________________

Second Child ____________________________________

Third Child _____________________________________

I had these problems during my pregnancy

First Child ______________________________________

Second Child ____________________________________

Third Child _____________________________________

Names we picked

Boy ____

Girl ____

The funniest part of my pregnancy was when

First Child

____

____

____

Second Child

____

____

____

Third Child

____

____

____

It was so exciting having a child, but having all these emotions all at once can be overwhelming. Here are some of my thoughts when you were just born.

____

____

____

____

____

____

____

____

When I brought you home from the hospital, we had quite a time. Let me tell you!

First Child ____

____

Second Child ____

____

Third Child ____

____

When I was raising my child(ren), times were

____

____

____

The golden rule I taught my child(ren) was

____

____

____

Now my child(ren) live(s)

____

____

____

We see them

____

____

____

MORE TO ADD ABOUT MY SECOND MARRIAGE AND FAMILY

Your life is
a story,
let people
learn from it.

RETIREMENT

Ahh . . . all these years, I waited for this moment!
I can do whatever I want. I can travel and
see the world or just relax and enjoy life!
I love this stage of my life—so many options!

I retired when I was ______ years old

My plans when I retired were

____

____

____

Since retirement, I ____

____

____

This is where I've volunteered my time

____

____

____

I plan on traveling to

____

____

____

Other things I am doing until we travel are

____

____

____

Throughout our life we have traveled, visiting these places

____

____

____

____

____

____

____

____

____

____

____

____

____

____

____

____

____

Things I want to learn or do now that I have retired!

Circle or underline the ones that interest you.

Activism
Amateur Radio
Antiquing
Aquariums
Archery
Art
Astronomy
ATVs
Badminton
Baking
Baton twirling
Baseball
Basketball
Beekeeping
Beach clean-up
Biking
Birding
Board games
Book club
Boomerangs
Brewing Beer
Bridge
Calligraphy
Camping
Cartooning
Casinos
Chess
Collage
Collecting
Composing Music
Cooking
Crafting
Crochet
CrossFit
Crossword puzzles
Dancing
Darts
Daydreaming
DJ
Drone Kits
Electronics
Entertaining
Fashion design

Fencing
Fishing
Flower arranging
Football
Flying
Four wheeling
Genealogy
Geocaching
Geology
Golf
Hot air balloons
Hiking
Horses
Hunting
Inventing
Jewelry making
Joining a Band
Journaling
Juggling
Kayaking
Kites
Knitting
Letter writing
Mahjong
Make movies
Marathons
Martial Arts
Metal Detecting
Mixology
Museums
Models
Motorcycles
Mycology-mushrooms
Orienteering
Origami Art
Paintball
Painting
Paragliding
Playing an Instrument
Photography
Ping pong
Poker
Pottery

Puppetry
Reading
Remote control cars
Road trips
Rock climbing
Robotics
Roller skating
Rowing
Running
Sailing
Sandcastles
Scuba
Sculpting
Senior Olympics
Sewing
Singing in a choir
Skiing
Snorkeling
Snowboarding
Soccer
Socializing
Storm chasing
Swimming
Surfing
Tai Chi
Tennis
Theater tryouts
Trampolines
Topiary
Upcycling
Volleyball
Watercolors
Wine making
Wine tasting
Woodshop
Wood carving
Writing
Yoga
Yoyos
Ziplining
Zoology
Zumba

MORE TO ADD ABOUT RETIREMENT

Getting old
is a trap!
I will be young
forever!

I AM NOT FINISHED WORKING YET!

So many of us don't want to stop working.
We love the interaction with people
and a job gives us a different purpose in life.

I kept working until I was ______ years of age

I worked at these companies after I retired from my career

____

____

I will tell you about the job I loved doing after I retired from my career

____

____

Most of my friends were retired, but I kept working. Let me tell you about this company and my position

____

____

If I had all of the money I wanted, this is what I would be doing

____

____

By the end of my life, it is my wish to accomplish

____

____

This is the career I wished I would have picked

____

____

When I finally retire and don't have to work any longer, this is what I want to do

____

____

____

____

____

My wishes for the end of my life are

____

____

____

____

____

____

____

FAVORITES

Some people love to name their favorite things.
Here's your chance to list them all!

	Younger Years	Adult Years
Holiday		
Hobby		
Board game		
Card game		
Dance		
Food		
Drink		
Color		
Park		
Animal		
Author		
Book/Novel		
Poem		
Play		
Singer		
Indoor activity		
Outdoor activity		
Song		
Musician		
Symphony		
Opera		

FAVORITES

*Some people love to name their favorite entertainment figures, etc.
Here's your chance to list them all!*

	Younger Years	**Adult Years**
Actor		
Actress		
Comedian		
TV Show		
Cartoon character		
Movie		
Vacation spot		
Place to go		
Spectator sport		
Athlete		
Sports team		
Saying		
Charity		
Way to travel		
Radio program		
Radio station		

MORE TO ADD ABOUT MY FAVORITES

*I am inserting this
COVID-19 section,
as the world is so
different now because of it.*

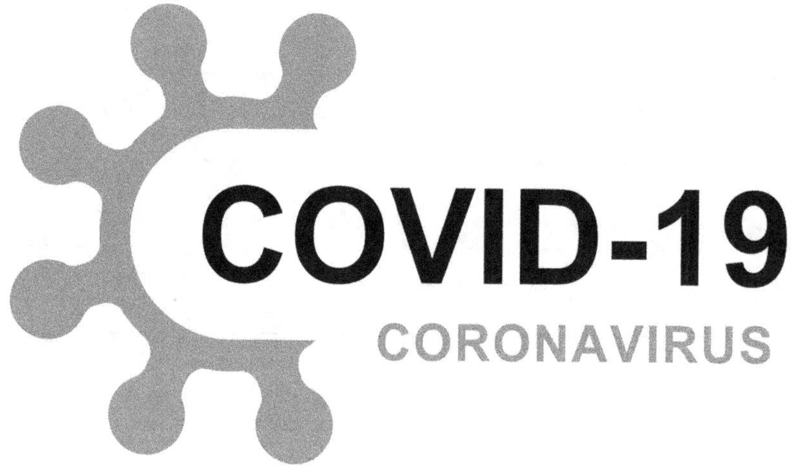

COVID-19 (SIP) SHELTER IN PLACE

In 2020 the United States and other parts of the world shut down.
We all had to live a new normal.
Explain what you went through and how you came out of it.

Our city ordered us to "SIP" Shelter in Place (Month/Year) ___________________

Last day of my SIP (Month/Year) ____

We had to "SIP" again (Month/Year) _____________________________________

Last day of my SIP (Month/Year)

____

Staying at home the first month was

____

____

I was at home a total of ______ days/weeks

These are the home projects I or my family did while sheltering at home

____

____

____

____

What we did daily

____

We had so much fun doing

____

____

____

____

I learned how to

____

____

I still never got to

____

____

During the pandemic

☐ I worked

☐ I was furloughed

☐ I was laid off

☐ I worked from home

I [   ] did [   ] did not get employment

Other _______________________________________

While I worked from home, my new office area

____

____

My new dress code during SIP was

____

____

New routines or rituals that I started

____

____

I [liked] or [did not like] working from home

Weirdest day I have had yet

____

____

____

Best day I have had yet

____

____

____

After we were at home for a few months life started getting

____

____

Things I was able to do during SIP

____

____

____

Things I was not able to do during SIP

____

____

____

This is who was with me during SIP

____

____

Games and fun activities we created for ourselves

____

____

____

Good things that came out of this pandemic

____

____

____

Events that went on during this pandemic

____

____

____

These sad events happened during this pandemic

____

____

____

Events I participated in during this pandemic

____

____

____

Lessons I have learned during this time

____

____

____

____

____

If you have kids

My day to day with the kids

____

____

____

Funny stories

____

____

____

This is how I kept the kids entertained during the day, evenings, and weekends?

____

____

____

Let me tell you how our children adapted to homeschooling.

____

____

____

____

____

____

WHAT HAVE YOU BEEN DOING MORE OF?

*(i.e., Baking, Crafts, Home Projects, Exercising,
Binge-watching TV, etc.)? Want to share any recipes?*

MORE TO ADD ABOUT COVID-19

My Story
Is NOT
over yet!

A LETTER TO MY FUTURE GENERATIONS

I am writing this to you now to tell you a few things I have been thinking about

A LETTER TO A LOVED ONE WHO HAS PASSED

I am writing you to tell you my feelings

I WOULD LIKE TO ADD

I WOULD LIKE TO ADD

**THE BLANK PAGES AHEAD ARE
FOR YOU TO PASTE PICTURES,
COLOR, USE STICKERS OR
WHATEVER YOU FEEL YOU
WANT TO SHARE**